MW01288565

HOW TO OVERCOME HEARTBREAK

Recovering from Misguided Love

Nicole D. Miller, MBA

Copyright © 2014 Nicole D. Miller
All rights reserved.

ISBN: 1499596731
ISBN 13: 9781499596731

This book is dedicated to my Father, who met me when I was immersed in darkness and pain. He took my pain and made it into something beautiful. To those who are weighed down with a broken heart, your time has come for healing. To the community that surrounded me in my time of need, your love, support, and patience have made me into the woman I am today.

"The Lord is near the brokenhearted."

—Psalm 34:18

TABLE OF CONTENTS

CHAPTER 1
THE BETRAYAL

"I'm seeing someone else, and I've been seeing her for a while. Every day this week that you haven't heard from me, I was talking to her."

Those were the words that pierced my ear and my heart. They were coming through the phone from the man who had been the love of my life for the last three years.

"What?" was pretty much all I could get out. The details of the conversation were a blur due to my high emotions. I was overcome with helplessness and confusion, and I'm pretty sure the room was spinning. I looked up at the ceiling of my on-campus, single dorm room at Miami University. *God, what is going on?* I thought.

I focused back on the conversation. Desperately but unsuccessfully I attempted to reason with him, saying something to the effect of "We're engaged. We're in love. What the heck are you thinking?" But no amount of reasoning would alter the fact that his feelings toward me had changed.

"Nicole, don't put your trust in man," said the cold, distant voice on the line. I was not familiar with that particular passage of Scripture at the time, but I soon would become very acquainted with its meaning.

We ended the conversation, and I sat on my bed for hours. I never had felt so alone in my life. I was twenty years old, a junior in college, and up until that point, I had felt pretty secure about my future. The plan was that after I finished my degree, I would marry this man, to whom I had pretty much dedicated the last few years of my life. We would conquer the world together and live happily ever after. But given that he was breaking up with me, that plan was in serious jeopardy, and I was left wondering, *What does my life amount to now?*

The next few days, I went through the motions of getting dressed, going to class, and carrying out my various academic-leadership roles. I felt as if I were little more than a wandering soul, weighed down by a broken heart. Creating journal entries for my accounting class seemed far less important than the never-ending ache in my chest, and yet I was still a student.

The world at large had not stopped turning just because my own small world had. So in order to cope, I did what any good Christian girl would do in my situation: I prayed.

I prayed for God to restore what apparently was being stolen from me. *God!* I cried. *Don't take him from me!* Silence. No audible voice, no flickering of the lights. I lay there, my face sunken into the coarse, five-by-eight-foot carpet I had purchased from Walmart my freshman year. My limbs were spread askew; I didn't have the strength to be on my knees. Salty, bitter tears painted my wet, chocolate face. Yet I still believed in God. I still believed that He was real and that He had heard me and that He was with me, even if He didn't answer. He was going to be my best bet for me not to sink deep down into that cheap carpet.

During my sophomore year, I had dedicated my life to Christ. Around the same time, my ex had as well, which signified to me that we were destined to be together. We shared a common thirst for God and a desire to share His word with any passersby. I had not been raised in church, but I was taught at a young age that God was real. I had found what some would term a personal relationship with Him, and at the age of nineteen, I had surrendered my life to Him. Little did I know that act of faith would not only promise me eternal life but also would be the rock I needed to stand on when this particular storm engulfed me.

My faith, as sustaining as it was, could not protect me from experiencing the effects of a broken heart. Due to intentional fasting and a complete lack of appetite, my weight started to drop. I cared little about my appearance. Every morning I was faced with the reality that the sudden turn of events in my life was not just an elaborate dream. If only it was! I would have pinched myself instantly if it would have helped me escape the hell I'd suddenly found myself in. Escapism was so appealing that suicide would have been an option, if I had not clung to the hope that God would get me through this time. Even so, the depths of despair that engulfed me made me want to escape not only from the situation but also from myself. At the same time, I felt as if I had lost myself. It is one of the most emotionally painful feelings in the world to feel as if you have lost yourself. I never had felt this way before about anyone or anything in my life. Was this normal?

Judging from the lyrics of popular ballads such as Lauryn Hill's "The Ex Factor," Alicia Keys's "Fallin'," and Taylor Swift's "Last Kiss," when you give your heart to someone, it takes the endurance, strength, and discipline of climbing Mount Everest to get it back. Somewhere along the way, that person became your life. Your life seems over, because when the person you love walks out the door, they take every moment you ever gave them right along with them. Every long conversation, every invested emotion, and every shared experience is gone. And in its place is a resounding echo of nothingness, as the door shuts closed behind them. If you were physically intimate with your significant other, there are now soul ties that make you feel as if your other half is gone (Gen. 2:24). You now feel as if you are no longer a whole person.

I don't believe anyone can know how deeply he or she felt about a person until that person is removed from his or her life. The degree of pain varies from one person to the next, but across the board, there is one thing that everyone needs for healing to occur. That one thing is time. That is what it took for me. That is what I'm certain it will take for you.

Reflection Questions

1. Have you ever felt that your happiness and success in life were dependent upon another person?

2. Which events in your life helped mold and shape your belief that your life's happiness is dependent upon your having a romantic relationship?

3. Do you still have the mind-set that you need a relationship in order to be successful and happy?

CHAPTER 2

THE GRAY PERIOD

One thing I've noticed is that when a long-term relationship ends, there is usually a period of time when the participating parties have not fully let go of the relationship. More than likely you will find yourself still in some type of communication with your ex after the breakup. The two of you may not technically have the title of "boyfriend and girlfriend," but you are still emotionally, mentally, and maybe even physically involved with your ex—and even possibly with his or her family. I call this period the "gray period," because things tend to look a little hazy during this time. You and your ex may have broken up, but your heart is not completely ready to sever all ties, so you're still involved.

It's OK if you're in this place, because if you desire to really be free from brokenness, you won't stay there. I personally found myself in this gray period for almost a year, which just goes to show that it really can take time to let go and move on. After the initial breakup, my ex and I did reunite—but as much as I wanted to hold on to our love, deep down I knew our time together had passed. We both had made some very hurtful choices from which I felt we were not going to be able to bounce back from together. Of course it took me a while to admit this truth to myself. During the initial stage of the "gray period," I held on to the hope that we would push through our challenges and remain together.

One thing that helped me transition from being in the "gray period" to completely severing all ties was that I was carving out a new life for myself, outside of him. We had been in a long-distance relationship, so that helped tremendously. I had developed very deep, life-giving relationships in college, and they proved to be essential to my healing process. The time I had dedicated to my previous relationship was now being filled with these friendships as well as with my schoolwork and extracurricular activities. Even so, immediately after the breakup, it often was excruciatingly painful to carry out those duties. I never had been one to listen to music while studying, as I found it distracting; however, while I was recovering from heartbreak, music helped dull the pain and also helped me focus on my studies. I fell in love with Shane & Shane's song "Be Near," and it was constantly on repeat. The lyrics spoke to the depths of my soul, as I felt I desperately needed God to be near.

Another way in which I developed my own life for myself was to take a missionary trip. This trip helped me focus on something other than myself and my conflicting emotions and thoughts. The gray period is full of confusion because your desires and feelings oppose what you know you *should* do. You *should* completely cut this person out of your life, but your heart is not ready. The missionary trip I took proved to be a great solution to help me clear my head of this confusion. It also helped me distance myself physically. When you're trying to move forward from the gray period, it's necessary to minimize contact with your ex. In some cases you may have to see your ex at a work establishment, church, or other key place in your life; however, if you feel that you are ready to let go of the relationship but don't feel strong enough to do it, frequent contact with your ex will not strengthen you. It will in fact weaken your resolve. Prayerfully consider going to a different church-service time or a different church altogether. This change may be necessary in your journey to heal, even if it's implemented only temporarily.

Creating physical distance proved to be a lifesaver for me. I not only developed new, healthy relationships on this missionary trip, but I also was able to grow spiritually, which further strengthened my resolve to move forward toward God's purposes for me. My newfound strength helped me remove myself emotionally and not communicate with my ex.

This is the time when it's vital for you to discover that you have an identity apart from your previous relationship. That will be an underlying theme in the initial stages of your healing and well into the rest of your life. Discovering who you are and your life's purpose is a journey. Being healed from heartbreak can prove to be a diamond hidden in the rough of that journey. Similar to this diamond, your healing may take time to find, but its value is well worth the search.

Reflection Questions

1. In which ways do you recognize that you are in a gray period with your ex?
2. What is making it hard for you to move forward from this place?
3. Do you have a support system in place to help you to move forward?
4. Which activities and programs can you become involved in that will help you in your healing process?

CHAPTER 3
THE NEW NORMAL

It may seem weird to be alone when you are used to being a part of a pair. Use that unsettled feeling to immerse yourself in a healthy community of people who want to know you for you and not for who you are with. You also may feel unsettled because you don't know who you are for yourself. You spent so much time with your ex that you took on his or her preferences, tastes, and character traits. This is natural. We do this often with friends and even more so with romantic partners. The people you now choose to surround yourself with will help you adjust to your new way of life. Women love to process verbally, and there is an understanding among friends that the brokenhearted will mention the old beau's name many times a day for a period of time. But that's OK, because one day those conversations will cease, and it will feel odder to mention your ex than not to mention him (or her if you're a guy).

After graduating from Miami University, I officially broke things off with my ex and found myself living a new life on all accounts. I was no longer a student and no longer a "girlfriend." I was simply Nicole—but still I didn't yet know who Nicole was. I also did not have a job, and I was living with my mom again—every college grad's fear. That was a rough season for me, because I was so used to being busy and active on campus. Now I spent my days fervently looking for a job and being frustrated when my searches came up empty. Everything I previously had used to define myself was now gone.

In hindsight I realize that was just the way God wanted it to be. I come from a long line of hardworking, strong, independent women who raised me to be the same. Yet those same character traits were hindering me from developing a deeper dependency on God. I found myself "kicking against the goads" (Acts 26:14) and did not understand at the time that my plan was once again different than God's. Fortunately I found a church to call home and received the unconditional love of men and women who saw me as a valuable gift to the body of Christ. I was actively involved in youth ministry and evangelism. This church became an outlet for me to use my gifts and talents, some of which I didn't even know existed prior to my participation in these ministries.

I greatly benefited from the part of my community that consisted of older leaders and mentors. So often youth think they know more than they really do. Even now I struggle with that mind-set! As I get older I'm learning that my elders really do have wisdom gained from their having lived a lot longer than me.

During my time of recovery, I had some great spiritual leaders in my life. We didn't just talk at church—we did things together. I was often at people's houses, with their kids, around their families, just hanging out. I desperately needed that. I had a huge hole in my heart, and being with others proved to be instrumental in closing it up.

I was finding my purpose slowly but surely. The ache in my heart was still there, but I knew I had to keep moving forward. Eventually I did find a job, which encouraged me that I was on the right path, as I felt God Himself had opened that door. Things were looking up. Healing was flowing into my heart amid the love and support that surrounded me in my newfound community. My mom and I had settled into our new life at home together, but I would soon learn that the battle for my healing was not over. I was hit with another fiery dart of the evil one (Eph. 6:16), and it was just as painful as the initial betrayal. It was around this time that I learned—a mere four months after our four-year relationship had ended—that my ex was getting married to another woman.

Reflection Questions

1. Are there other things you have used in your life to define your worth or identity besides your relationship?
2. Do you feel you have a good sense of self and identity? If not, how can you obtain this?
3. In which ways can you seek out older mentors and leaders in your life?

CHAPTER 4

SO YOUR EX HAS MOVED ON

The media is notorious for promoting the "moving on to the next" syndrome. From Rihanna to John Mayer, the role models for today's youth mostly demonstrate that the best way to get over an old love is to get a new one. "Out with the old, in with the new" is the motto of today. Hollywood actually applauds such scenarios, coining cute nicknames such as "Brangelina." At best there will be very little time between the new and old relationships for these famous couples. At worst the new relationships will overlap the old ones. Sadly this way of life only allows the participating parties to accumulate a host of baggage to their souls. This baggage consists of pain, mistrust, and bitterness—all of which are carried from one relationship to the next.

Often when the brokenhearted person jumps into a new relationship, he or she will either consciously or subconsciously make the new love pay for the old love's actions. This results in additional pain, and if the new love is also wounded, the new relationship is just a time bomb waiting to explode. Yet this option of "on to the next" seems to be preferred by many at the culmination of a relationship, probably because it appears to be easier. Appearances, however, can be deceiving. People were created to be fulfilled by their Creator yet often try to fulfill themselves with creation. That is what is happening when one does not choose to heal from heartbreak and instead takes up a new romance prematurely. The new relationship is an attempt to fill the emptiness the person now feels as a result of his or her ex no longer being a part of his or her life. Do yourself a favor and let the Creator—and not the creation—fill this emptiness. It will save you a great deal of unnecessary pain and eliminate a lot of wasted time.

It was the middle of the night. I was tossing and turning on my bedroom floor, and I couldn't sleep. That day I had found out through mutual friends that my ex was engaged. I felt as if I had been slapped in the face. Not only was he dating, but he also was engaged.

How did he move on so soon? I thought. *Did he even love me at all?* My heart cried out in agony, and I curled into a fetal position, burying my head into the pillow. *God, help me!*

I continued to toss and turn until finally I moved to the living room, stretched out on the couch, and continued my attempt at rest. There it was again: that desire to escape from my own self. But I couldn't escape. I was going to have to find a way to walk this out. Eventually I fell asleep, but I awoke to the reality that I was still brokenhearted. I proceeded with my new routine. I processed my pain with the friends and mentors who surrounded me. I prayed. I walked forward, one step at a time—until another hard day came: his wedding day.

I was at a baby shower for mutual friends of ours. Through these friends I had become aware that my ex was to be married that evening. When I saw some of them leave the shower, I knew they were leaving to attend his wedding. I sat there feeling empty, just trying to keep it together. Then I felt the Lord's Spirit.

Nicole, God said, *if you wait, you will have My best.* Up until this season of my life, I hadn't had to wait for anything. I had experienced the gifts of God, His love, His presence, and His goodness—you know, the "fun" stuff. He had immersed me in a great community and answered even my smallest prayers; however, now I was facing trials and heartbreak. On top of that, God was asking me to wait.

In retrospect I see the importance of waiting. Waiting brings forth significant character traits such as patience and endurance. Yet I did not choose to wait in order to obtain maturity in these areas. I waited simply because God wanted me to. God was in fact the sole reason I had ended things with my ex. He told me to lay down the relationship, and for the first time in my life, I found someone I loved even more than my man. I loved Jesus. God in His goodness knew that although I desired to do His will, I would need His strength to actually fulfill it.

That night I clung to God's words in my heart. God promised me His best if I trusted Him and walked forward into the new life that was before me. This required great faith on my part. The circumstances I found myself in made me feel like a loser, not a winner. I had given my heart to a man who betrayed me, and he ended up marrying someone else. So often, when you are following God's way, it will seem as if you are losing. It will seem as if those who betrayed you are victorious and are receiving the very things you want for yourself. In the Bible the story of Joseph is a perfect example of this.

Joseph was betrayed by his brothers and sold into slavery because they envied him. As a slave he was humbled and worked hard for his master, Potiphar. He was elevated in Potiphar's house and had authority over all. Just when things seemed to be turning around for him, he was accused of having seduced his master's wife (when in fact it was the other way around). As a result of this false accusation, Joseph was thrown into jail for three long years. Afterward he was freed and elevated once again—talk about an emotional roller-coaster ride—this time by the ruler of the Egyptians, Pharaoh.

Prior to these events, God had promised Joseph that he would rule over his brothers one day. However, God did not inform Joseph of the journey he would embark on before the fruition of this promise; he did not tell him that in fact it was the journey itself that would prepare him to be the ruler God had called him to be. Having been betrayed by his own family, enslaved by his enemies, lied about by his master's wife, and imprisoned for a crime he did not commit, Joseph understood pain. He understood feeling like a loser. His brothers had gotten rid of him. They were living it up in their hometown, while he was being brought to the very end of himself. But even in his darkest hours, his brothers were not privy to the humiliation he felt. God used Joseph's enslavement to separate him from his brothers and hide him away in the shadow of His wings.

I too have experienced this type of protection from God. On the inside I was fighting each day to move forward and live life, but on the outside, to those who opposed me, it seemed as if I were doing just fine. An example of this was the day I was to face my ex and his wife. I actually had no intention of attending this particular gathering but was led by the Holy Spirit to do so. Sometimes God leads us to do things that are painful because it is an opportunity for Him to show His strength in the very areas in which we are weak. A great example of this occurred when Jesus was led into the wilderness by the Holy Spirit during his forty-day fast and was tempted by Satan (Matt. 4:1). The Holy Spirit did not tempt Jesus Himself but led Jesus to a place where He would be in a physically weakened state and the power of God would shine through Him.

Similarly I was led to a Christian concert that many of my friends were attending. When I walked into the building, I felt empowered. I spotted my ex and his wife to my right and kept my face straight ahead, my head held high. I quickly made my way to my seat in the midst of friends and focused on the performance. I tried my best but could not stop my body from physically responding. My hands were shaking; my stomach felt queasy; and I was afraid I was going to vomit. I typed out a quick text message to my three best friends, informing them of my condition and requesting prayer. They responded immediately, and I'm sure it was their prayers that strengthened me that night.

You see, not only did I have to be near my ex for the first time since our breakup, but I also had to watch him perform, as he was one of the acts in the concert. Additionally I witnessed a wedding proposal during a break in the performance. A well-intentioned young man got down on one knee and asked for his lady's hand in marriage. The audience broke out in applause and surrounded him with congratulations. It was everything I could do to keep a fake smile on my face. Inside I felt awful. I was brokenhearted, newly single, and in the presence of my ex and his wife, while someone else was being proposed to. I felt like sinking down low in my seat, but the Holy Spirit didn't allow that. When God's name is on the line, He will make sure His children look good too. So I kept my composure, socialized with my friends, and made it through the night without shedding a tear—in fact without saying a word. Christ did not say a word as His persecutors mocked Him and beat Him. God was using this event to cultivate the same meekness in my own character. If it had been up to me, I would not have attended the event and would have kept my distance from my ex, but God had other plans. When I asked God why He was adamant about my staying in the same city as my ex, when it was my desire to relocate, he said to me very clearly, *Nicole, I will set a table before you in the presence of your enemies.*

It may be hard to believe when someone has betrayed you, but the truth of the matter is that people are not the enemy. Our real enemy is spiritual, because we do not wrestle against flesh and blood but against spiritual hosts of wickedness in heavenly places (Eph. 6:12). Once we have this understanding, we can fight with spiritual weaponry such as prayer, fasting, and communion with God instead of retaliating with unkind words and gestures. So God was not stating that my ex was the enemy, He was stating that by keeping me in proximity to the one who had betrayed me, through my obedience, humility, and faith, He would use me to show my spiritual enemies His own strength. He would use me to be a testimony of His own hand.

To believe that a person is the enemy is a false belief, rooted in hurt. People are people. They are not perfect, and often when others hurt you, it is because *they* are hurt. There is a saying I completely agree with: "Hurting people hurt people." I had hurt my ex by breaking up with him the second time around, and his actions caused hurt to me because I still cared for him. Having that understanding helped me greatly in dealing with the unexpected turn of events in my life. I had made the mistake of putting my trust in man. This is not to say that we are not to trust others, but we are to trust people to be people, not to be perfect. This experience taught me that I could trust only God to be perfect and never to intentionally hurt me. I could not even put trust in myself and believe that I was able to recover from this situation alone. I had to depend solely on Christ's guidance—even if it meant Christ would guide me on the road less taken, which in this case meant not jumping into the next relationship that came along. It also meant remaining in the same city as my ex and even among the same community of people for a time.

God's will is different for everyone. Sometimes He will physically remove us from those we were romantically involved with. I have friends who have this testimony, and I have even experienced this with other relationships. It's important for you to know if you are called to relocate physically or if you are to remain where you are. Either way know that God's choice for you is the best choice, even when it doesn't appear to be.

Thus far His road for me did not appear to be the best. I was now single and brokenhearted, and my ex was newly married. Additionally I harbored a fear of running into him and his wife at any moment. Little did I know I definitely would have to face that fear, as that first meeting would not be our last.

Reflection Questions

1. How can waiting to heal before beginning a new relationship benefit your new relationship in the long run?

2. Do you believe God has a better plan for you than what you have experienced with this breakup?
3. How can this breakup be a part of the journey God has put you on to fulfill your ultimate purpose?

CHAPTER 5
THE SECRET TO HEALING

Early on in my brokenhearted state, I understood that I needed to forgive. I understood that it was necessary for me to walk in freedom from bitterness and anger and that forgiving the one who had betrayed me would be instrumental in my healing. I still cared a great deal about my ex and wanted the best for him. I did not want to feel animosity toward him and in fact still had a desire for us to continue a friendship. You may be struggling with forgiving your ex because all you can feel is the pain he or she inflicted upon you. Give yourself time, and even if you are unable to forgive, pray for the ability to forgive. It is for your own good.

Forgiveness unlocks the door to an abundant life. Christ's ability to forgive the very ones who nailed Him to the cross is a great illustration of that. Three days after His death, He resurrected and had the power to give this eternal life to others, including those who had betrayed him. His love and forgiveness led to freedom for all who wanted it. If we choose not to forgive, the heaviness of resentment will weigh down even the most carefree spirit. There is no way we can experience continual joy and love if we have unforgiveness in our hearts.

One thing that helped me to forgive was reminding myself that God had forgiven me for all my sins. If I chose to harbor unforgiveness, I was saying I was greater than God, who forgives all. Forgiveness is a conscious decision; it's not a feeling or emotion. One does not forgive because one is in the mood to forgive. If we waited to be in the mood to do anything Christlike, we never would do anything Christlike.

Even though I had forgiven my ex, there was another area in my heart I was overlooking that was preventing my full healing from manifesting. That area was one of entitlement. Entitlement is rooted in pride because it makes people feel as if they have the right to something. At the time I felt I had the right to cheat on my ex after he had cheated on me. When we are in pain, we have a choice of whether we will process that pain in an unhealthy manner or in a healthy manner.

By cheating on my ex, I chose to process it in an unhealthy manner. Thankfully, eventually I did choose healthier options that led to my healing.

I'll never forget the day I was sitting in my mom's kitchen, devouring a book about relationships. It had been more than a year since my breakup, and I was still struggling with feeling hurt and wounded, still fighting thoughts about my ex every day, and still carving out a life for myself. Then my eyes fell on a page that discussed how the author had received healing by forgiving the person who had hurt her. Well, I already had forgiven my ex. However, what I did not understand was that God now wanted me to request forgiveness *from* my ex.

Nicole, you need to ask him *for forgiveness.* I heard the Holy Spirit say this to me in my heart clearer than I could have heard Him say it aloud.

It was so clear that I responded verbally to the seemingly empty room, "Ask him forgiveness for what?" I was shocked that God could think that I— hands-down the *victim* in the situation—needed to request forgiveness.

Well, before I could even huff and puff over it, I heard His response immediately: *For betraying* him. God brought to my remembrance some very hurtful things I did to my ex after the breakup.

My response to God was, "But he betrayed me first!" Here I was, having a verbal dialogue with the

Alpha and Omega, and all I could do was defend myself and point the finger.

God, in His love and mercy, patiently responded to me, *Sin is never justified, Nicole.*

Now that was a shocker. God was telling me that even though in my mind I had hurt my ex because he first had hurt me, my actions were still sinful. My attempt at retaliation was not overlooked by God just because I was acting out of hurt. Basically two wrongs do not make a right. And so, once I let that little nugget of truth digest in my heart, I saw the need for me to apologize to the one I had hurt. What I did not realize at the time was that in making that decision to apologize, I was humbling myself. I was choosing to accept responsibility for my own actions and not put the blame on someone else.

In the Garden of Eden, we see how Adam and Eve pointed fingers. Adam blamed Eve, and Eve blamed the serpent. But what would have happened if Adam and Eve had taken responsibility for their individual mistakes? What if they chose instead to repent to God for their own wrongdoings? How would future generations of their lineage have been affected? How will yours be if you take responsibility for your mistakes? God draws near to those who humble themselves and will not despise a broken, and contrite heart (Ps. 51:17).

I ended up asking my ex for forgiveness at a mutual friend's wedding shortly after my verbal conversation with the Lord. Both he and his wife were in attendance. So my fear of seeing them both was coming to pass; however, this time I was looking forward to the meeting. As awkward and hard as this would be for me, I pushed forward and had a one-on-one with my ex, requesting his forgiveness. I wanted my healing more than I wanted anything else, and I didn't care what it took to get it. There was desperation in my heart, similar to that of the woman in the Bible who bled for twelve years. She was so desperate to touch just the hem of Jesus's robe and receive her healing that she pushed her way through the masses and even risked infecting others with her defilement. The Jewish customs required a period of cleansing for anyone she came in contact with. Jesus Himself would have been at risk to be defiled according to Jewish laws, yet this woman's faith was so great that she knew that instead of her defiling Him, He would heal her.

I by no means can take credit for the bravery and humility I was displaying. It was truly a work the Holy Spirit was doing in my heart, and even though it was difficult, I am the better for it.

There have been other relationships in my life that have caused me to either forgive or ask for forgiveness. These situations have taught me that forgiveness is a reliable source of healing and freedom. You may not need to have a one-on-one, face-to-face meeting or even a telephone conversation with your ex to forgive him or her. It is only important that you make the decision to forgive the person in your heart. Once you've made that decision, I guarantee your healing will flow.

Questions to Ask Yourself to Help Recognize Unforgiveness in Your Heart

1. Do you become angry, upset, bitter, jealous, or experience any other negative emotion when you think about the one who offended you?
2. Are you unable to speak about the one who offended you in a positive manner?
3. Do you desire harm to come to the one who offended you?
4. Are you unable to interact with the one who offended you without harboring negative feelings toward him or her?

CHAPTER 6
WHAT LED TO THE BREAKUP?

Now is the time for us to do a little soul-searching. Like me, you may not have done anything to cause the breakup, but there may be some things in you that led you on the path to pain. For me one of those things was having a serious case of daddy issues. I grew up in a home where my mother and grandmother were my parents. My father left when I was a small child, and as a teenager, I turned to men to try to fill that void. Every relationship I pursued and became involved in was an attempt to receive the male attention I'd never had. A child is created to receive the love and affection of both the mother and father, so no matter how great the one parent is, there always will be something missing if both are not in the home and emotionally involved in raising the child.

I honestly did not feel as if I were missing anything while growing up. I was loved and taken care of, yet deep in my heart, I yearned to hear my father's voice. It wasn't until my college years that I began to awaken to the fact that I needed and desired to have my father in my life. Thankfully by then I had come to know God as my Heavenly Father. But because I desired that male attention so desperately as a teenager, I was idolizing it without realizing it.

In biblical days idolatry was pretty obvious. Don't worship a calf and you're safe! However, under the new covenant, we now have a greater revelation of idolatry and understand that it is all about the heart. Anything that we desire more than God is an idol. Unbeknown to me I already was idolizing men, so naturally once I fell in love, I idolized that relationship. The idolatry of that relationship caused me to worship it. I worshiped my ex and who we were together. Our relationship became the most important thing in the world to me, and that was the main reason the breakup was so hard on me. I had lost the most precious thing to me when my ex and I broke up. I did not know how to function without it. You may not have daddy issues, but you may be able to relate to the fact that your previous relationship consumed too much of your time and energy. Could it be because you put the relationship into a place in your heart that should be reserved only for your Creator? Here are a few questions to ask yourself to see if you have idolized your relationship:

1. Do I have obsessive thoughts about this person?
2. Do/did I consistently choose to spend time with him or her rather than family members and other loved ones?
3. Do I feel devastated when I think about this person no longer being in my life? Suicidal even?

While dating my ex, I once had a dream in which I was being chased by someone who was attempting to kill me. I woke up from the dream in a panic; it seemed so real that it took me a while to realize it was only a dream. As I awoke the only thing I could think was that I could not afford to die because my ex needed me. I didn't think about any other family member or friend but him. I now see that my response was due to idolatry. At that time my sole purpose for wanting to live was for my boyfriend. We never should base our life's purpose on another individual. We should have a resolute mind to live only for God.

Having daddy issues was not the only obstacle I faced as a teenager. I also struggled with an eating disorder. This eating disorder deceived me into believing that I had control over my life. There were many other things happening at that time in my life that I could not control, so I turned to my diet instead. As with any addiction, I soon found that the very thing I thought I had control over now had control over me. On the outside I had achieved the weight I desired; however, I was on a constant roller coaster of overeating then purging what I ate. Inside I was crying out for help, but the cry never made it past my lips for others to hear. My self-perception was distorted. I looked in the mirror and thought my beauty was based on the size of my hips. I felt the only way I truly could be beautiful and attractive was to change my natural appearance.

This line of thinking is rooted in self-hatred. It's as if I were saying, "God, you made a mistake when You made me this way, and I need to correct Your mistake."

It is only now, more than a decade later, that I'm learning to love myself and what that means for me. There are plenty of self-help books out there that will claim to be able to show you the way to self-love, but the truth is that human love is insufficient to meet our need for love. If we attempt to love ourselves with our own human love, we will still feel dissatisfied. Only God's love can satisfy. My prayer these days is to love myself with God's perfect love. When people don't love themselves, they won't value themselves and will settle for any affection or attention they can get. In extreme cases such individuals will open the door to their heart to any passersby who come knocking. In less extreme cases, these individuals may overlook numerous red flags that are frantically waving back and forth as they attempt to hold on to unhealthy relationships, no matter the cost.

Loving yourself does not just mean you are comfortable spending time alone. I've been to my share of movies and dinners all by my lonesome yet have still found it difficult not to settle for the best romance God has for me. Part of loving yourself is having a revelation of your own intrinsic value. It is understanding deep in your heart that you are great and more than enough all by yourself. Before I met my ex, I did not have that understanding. I was desperately searching for something—anything—to make me feel whole, to make me feel great. In my searching I stumbled upon unhealthy, abusive behaviors that further propelled me into a downward spiral of self-loathing. This self-loathing was masked by my relationship. As long as I was part of a pair, I didn't have to look inside and acknowledge how wounded I felt as a single person.

In addition to my own personal struggles, my family history played a role in my poor decision-making skills in the area of love. Like many people I had few examples of healthy marriages to learn from. Instead fornication, adultery, physical abuse, sexual abuse, divorce, and the births of children out of wedlock were common occurrences in my family. Even if I never had physically witnessed these things, the fact that they had happened repeatedly had established the generational curses I was susceptible to, simply because of my DNA. Can you look at your own family history and see certain unhealthy patterns? Could your relationship be a replica of an older relative's unhealthy relationship? Feel free to read the prayer for breaking generational curses at the end of this chapter if you believe it is needed.

I have shared key factors that I believe contributed to my falling into an unhealthy relationship. You may or may not be able to relate to them; however, I encourage you to spend time in self-reflection to discover your own personal struggles that caused you to choose the wrong person to love. Receiving outside counseling may help you in this discovery. I also recommend reading the books *Boundaries* and *Safe People*, both by Dr. Henry Cloud and Dr. John Townsend, for a clearer understanding of what a healthy romantic relationship looks like.

The truth of the matter is the relationship you previously were in was doomed from the beginning, which is why it didn't last. If you do not mature in your needed areas, you will be destined to experience a broken heart all over again with someone new. The breakup was bound to happen because the foundation of the romance was not properly laid. God wants to properly lay the foundation in you so that next time around love will endure. And even more important, when the storms of life come, you will not falter but stand. Unshaken.

Prayer for Breaking Generational Curses

Father, I repent on behalf of my family for committing sins knowingly and unknowingly against You. I choose to live for You and to follow the path You have for me. I break all generational curses in my bloodline in the name of Jesus. I cover my bloodline in the blood of Jesus. Amen.

CHAPTER 7

LIVING SINGLE

By now you probably have realized that I am an advocate for taking out time for yourself to heal from heartbreak. Don't get me wrong—I do believe God can move speedily in bringing you the right relationship after you have ended the wrong one. I know couples who have had this experience, but as I learn and grow in God, I'm discovering the benefits of maturing as a single person. Taking time out for you makes it so much easier to discover who you are while single instead of in the midst of a relationship—and discovering who you are is essential to your calling and purpose on this earth. After all, no one can do what you do just the way you do it.

Sadly it seems to be a common occurrence for women to live as if their roles as mothers and wives are their whole identity. Then when the kids grow up—or God forbid the husband walks out—the woman is left wandering aimlessly, unsure of herself and in some cases unable to do things *for* herself. I would have been that woman if I had not pressed forward into God's plan for me. And in that pressing, I have learned and continue to learn that we are not human *doings*, we are human *beings*, meaning we are not what we do. What we do does not define us, but who we were originally intended to be is what matters.

To be clear, by pressing into my purpose, I mean that I quieted my spirit and followed the lead of the Holy Spirit. By spending time with God in prayer, I was able to discern what His will was for my life during that season. That way I would make decisions according to *His* desire and not my own. So in a sense, my action was birthed from a place of inaction. My doing stemmed from a place of being. Christ is the perfect example of this phenomenon. He was Spirit led in everything He did in His life, and He only did what He saw the Father doing in His intimate time spent in prayer. No more, no less. Some of the things Christ did caused the religious rulers of the day to condemn Him be-cause His actions did not line up with what was accept-able for religious people's behavior. They called Him a winebibber and a glutton because He drank wine and ate bread. They compared Him to John the Baptist, who did neither.

What these religious people did not understand—and what Christ did understand—was that Christ had a different purpose than John the Baptist. Because He knew that purpose, He was not bound to the conventions set for others. He was a trailblazer and on a totally different path than anyone who had walked before Him. And guess what? So are you. Just as the world was dependent on Christ's knowing His purpose and His being determined to pursue it, regardless of what others thought, it is just as vital for you to know and pursue yours.

Christ was the firstborn of many brethren (Rom. 8:29). He was the firstborn so that all others after Him could emulate His life and fulfill their destinies, just as He did. It may not seem fair, but currently your destiny involves being single. God may not have intended for you to be betrayed or brokenhearted, but He certainly worked it into His life plan for you, seeing as it has occurred. That means He also worked it into His plan for you to be single, even if temporarily.

My own season of singleness has lasted longer than I expected—nine years and counting as of the writing of this book. At the time of my breakup, I never could have dreamed of being single for nine years. I also never would have believed that I could live a life completely independent of my ex and that I no longer would be in love with him. What I didn't know then—and what I have come to learn—is that you change so much as you grow older. I started dating in my late teens and ended my relationship in my early twenties. I am now thirty-one and cannot even relate to the young woman I used to be. Sure, the core of who I am is the same. I am still tender-hearted, love music, and enjoy a good game night, but my convictions and world outlook have changed drastically. The memories I have from that time in my life play across my mind's eye, much like watching a movie. The audience of a movie tends to be objective and relate less emotionally to what's happening on the screen than the actors in the movie. The actors are a part of the scenes, whereas the audience is just watching. I'm so grateful to now be in the audience!

One important way that I have changed is that I now value myself so much more than I used to. I have higher standards for myself as well as for a potential mate. A huge factor in my growing awareness of my worth stems from my getting to know Christ. God does not throw Himself at people. One cannot experience His intimacy and friendship unless he or she first commits to having a relationship with Him. Commitment precedes intimacy with God, because He is valuable and He understands His value. This dynamic between commitment and intimacy holds true for His children.

As a teenager I did not understand how precious I was. I was unaware that my body and heart were of great value and should not be given away easily. I did not know that the only time to fully surrender those gifts to the man I love is on our wedding night.

Maybe you are like I was, in that you did not have that understanding, and now you are feeling the effects of having sex before having received a more solid commitment in the form of a wedding ring. If that is the case, then like me, you were duped by popular culture. As much as the media wants us to think otherwise, sex is not just a physical act. It is also emotional, spiritual, and mental. It encompasses our whole beings and cannot be compartmentalized from the rest of our lives. When a man and a woman unite physically, they become one in every way possible. Because I had been physically intimate in my relationship, I experienced a level of devastation once the relationship was over that I do not believe I would have experienced if we had not had sex. Thankfully I was knowledgeable about the creation of soul ties and received the deliverance needed to lessen the pain that soul ties cause in breakups. I have included a short prayer at the end of this chapter. If you would like to, feel free to pray this prayer to break any soul ties established during the physical consummation of your previous relationship.

If you were not physically intimate with your ex, it does not mean your pain is less severe. It is not wise to compare yourself to others. Your pain is your pain, and your experience is your experience. It is not better or worse than anyone else's—it is simply yours. It is my experience that you also can establish soul ties by being emotionally and mentally intimate with someone, not just physically. I also have used prayer to break soul ties that were established from unhealthy emotional connections with men. Feel free to pray this prayer for yourself if you feel it is needed.

Whether or not you were physically intimate with your ex, I'm sure you can look back and see mistakes that you made in other areas of your last relationship that contributed to your brokenheartedness. Let me give you a piece of valuable advice: don't beat yourself up for these mistakes, because God makes all things new. Every day we are given on this earth is a chance to start over, but it's really up to us to take it; for me, starting over meant living single.

During this time of singleness, not only have I gained a greater understanding of my worth and discovered more of my identity and life purpose, but also I have obtained the blessing of maturing in my character. The great thing about maturity is that it will aid you in not making the same mistakes over and over. For you that may mean not choosing the same type of good-for-nothing guy or girl again and again. This growth in character is so necessary because you can look good on the outside, but if your inside is the equivalent of a toddler's, more than likely you will only attract toddlers (boys who are not interested in becoming men or girls who are not interested in becoming women).

My best friend has the most beautiful three-year-old you've ever seen: caramel-brown skin; waist-length, curly, dark hair; and large brown eyes. When she smiles my heart melts, and I just want to give her everything under the sun. That being said, she is still your typical three-year-old. She throws tantrums, cries, and whines just like a toddler. Watching her parents in action during a recent visit, I realized that one of their greatest roles in her life is to build up her character. They teach her manners; they discipline her with time-outs; and they limit her ice-cream intake. They do these things because otherwise one day she would be a thirty-year-old, crying, whining adult with beautiful brown eyes, caramel skin, and flowing, dark hair. So even though I'm sure she hates the time-outs, they really are in her own best interest. Think of your time of singleness as being a time-out to work on yourself and grow in character.

When we go through life and choose the harder road, it cultivates our character. When we deny ourselves the desires of our hearts for God's best, we gain wisdom that can be attained only through taking the road less traveled. The single life has its ups and downs, just as marriage has its ups and downs. There may be evenings when you are tempted to drown your loneliness with a bottle of wine or fill your stomach with doughnuts, but that happens with or without a relationship. That happens in life. The hand you are dealt really just comes down to God's will for your life. As long as you are in His will, you can make it through the hardships that are set before you on your individual journey. As you withstand and overcome those hardships, you are working out and building up your muscle of endurance. And I promise you that weeping may endure for a night, but joy really does come in the morning (Ps. 30:5).

That being said, although both marriage and singleness have their challenges, these challenges differ greatly. Additionally, because you previously have given your heart away and maybe even your body, finding yourself single has its own unique challenges.

Early on in my singleness, although I did not struggle with loneliness, I did struggle with the desire for marriage. Love had been awakened prematurely, so now I had to figure out how to make it go back to sleep! There was a constant burning in my heart for marriage and for a husband. One great outlet for me was to journal about my experience during this time. Now, as I reread these journal entries, I see how God answered my prayers and how even my life circumstances were an answer. I prayed for more maturity and for a closer relationship with God. As I was discovering, a broken heart was the perfect opportunity to grow closer to Him!

As time went on, the burning in my heart for marriage eventually lessened; however, it has been a constant challenge for me to move forward in life while this desire has gone unmet. Although this desire was natural and given to me by God, the premature awakening of love, the false understanding of the purpose of marriage, and the generational curses that existed in my family all helped magnify this desire. This magnifying caused a constant war within my heart between the false illusions of what I thought marriage was and my choosing God's will to remain single, which seemed the less desirable of the two.

For most of my singleness, I was under the deception of what our culture teaches about the purpose of marriage. I truly believed that if I received my husband, marriage in some way would complete me and make me a whole person, as if I were lacking something. I now see that the deep longing I was experiencing was for intimacy with my Maker. I was confusing that longing for the natural desire for marriage God had given me. I also have come to understand that the purpose of marriage is to represent the relationship between Christ and His bride, a relationship rooted in selflessness.

This is contrary to the teachings of popular culture, which repeatedly sends the message that the purpose of marriage is to make us happy. Often when people enter their marriage believing this lie, they quickly call it quits once they are no longer happy. Those emotional highs that happen early on in the relationship seem to dissipate once two people say "I do" and begin to experience life together. The true purpose of marriage seems to be overshadowed by the false concept that it is supposed to make you happy and fulfill you. It wasn't until I received the knowledge of the true purpose of marriage that I had more understanding about God's purpose for my singleness. Not only was it to heal me, but it also was to lay a good foundation in my character so that one day I could experience a healthy, lasting marriage that would require a continual practice of selflessness. My ability to consistently deny myself these nine years, remain single, and choose God's will over my own not only has benefited me spiritually but also will benefit my future husband.

Thankfully, as a single person, I have not struggled too much with being lonely. There is a common misconception that if you are single, you are lonely. The truth is there are many married people who are lonely in their marriages. As I continue this journey, I'm seeing there are seasons to life, and some seasons may call one to be surrounded by people, whereas others may require times of solitude. If you do not know God as the source of your fulfillment, then even during those seasons of community, you can still feel alone. The times I have felt lonely have been due to my leaning on others as sources of fulfillment and then no longer having access to those people. Since God has promised that He never will leave us, the truth is that we are never alone. To not feel lonely, we must awaken to the truth that we are never alone.

One benefit I have that has helped me immensely is that most of my friends are single too, so I don't have to worry about feeling like the third wheel while constantly being surrounded by couples. Even so, there are couples in my life that provide me with needed fellowship and mentoring. It is important to have a good mix of couples and singles in your life so that you have a realistic view of marriage and an empathetic ear when you are struggling with your unmet desire. I'm grateful to have many people in my life who love and support me. Most weekends there is something to do and someone to see and spend time with. When there are times that are more mundane, I try to appreciate them, as I understand that life is full of busy seasons and slow seasons, whether or not one is in a relationship.

If you do not have a group of single and married friends, join a club or organization in which people have the same interests as you. That way you can meet a variety of people in a situation where the focus is not on your relationship status but on your common shared interest.

One of my passions is running. I love to run even though I'm not very fast. It is also a great time of devotion with the Lord. My spirit is at rest, and it's an effective stress reliever after a long day of sitting at work. Running also has proved to be a great emotional outlet when I struggle with being single. Those endorphins have a knack of eliminating feelings of depression.

These last nine years have taught me that life does not revolve around romantic relationships. Love and support should not be limited to just one relationship but need to be spread out among a community of people; otherwise we unknowingly will become too needy and too dependent on that one relationship. These nine years also have shown me that I can overcome things I never dreamed I would have to face. And if I can do it, you can too.

Prayers for Breaking Soul Ties

Father, I ask Your forgiveness for my engaging in physical intimacy with someone who is not my spouse. I see now that I have not treated my body with respect by doing so, and I understand that my body belongs to You. I receive Your forgiveness and ask that You would help me honor my body by helping me abstain from sex until marriage. I now break all ungodly soul ties I have established with (insert name of sexual partner) and renounce all actions consisting of sexual intimacy with (name of sexual partner) through the blood of Jesus. Thank You, Father, for completing the work You started in me and making me whole in You. Amen.

Father, I ask Your forgiveness for my engaging in an unhealthy emotional relationship with someone who is not my spouse. I see now that I have not treated my heart with respect by doing so, and I understand that my heart belongs to You. I receive Your forgiveness and ask that You would help me guard my heart until marriage, when I will be free to give it to my spouse. I now break all ungodly soul ties I have established with (insert name of partner) and renounce all actions that attributed to my establishing an unhealthy emotional relationship with (name of partner) through the blood of Jesus. Thank You, Father, for completing the work You started in me and making me whole in You. Amen.

Reflection Questions

1. In which ways can taking time out from dating and remaining single help you grow as a person?
2. Are there any lies or false illusions you have received from your culture about the purpose of marriage?
3. Do you see any false expectations that you had for marriage that resulted from these false illusions?
4. Which activities do you enjoy that can aid in your healing during this time of heartbreak?

CHAPTER 8

WHEN IS IT OK TO DATE?

OK, so you may be thinking, *Well, Nicole, activities, friends, and family are fine, but what about dating? When is it OK to **date**?*

That is a question only you can answer for yourself; however, I would advise you to make sure that you are healed before you start dating. Every person is different, and there is no recipe you can follow to be healed and start a new relationship. For me, dating multiple partners has not been appealing, nor do I feel that I could handle this type of casual dating that is seen frequently in popular culture. I'm a pretty sensitive person, so I get attached easily to others. In order for me to guard my heart, I do not casually date. Early on in my singleness, I actually went on a "dating fast." The book I was reading at the time encouraged refraining from dating to take time out to grow in God and focus on other aspects of life.

I was actually the last of my friends to do the fast and arguably the most affected by it. The fast lasted six months, and not only did I not date, but I also was very selective about speaking with male friends on the phone. It was during this fast that I realized I had a very unhealthy emotional relationship with a male friend. This friendship had been in place during my relationship with my ex, and I unknowingly became very dependent on this male friend and used him to fill the void that was in my heart after my breakup with my ex. This fast helped me see that although physical boundaries had not been crossed in this friendship, emotional boundaries had been, and I was in a full-fledged emotional affair. It took me years to break this off, and when I did, the pain was as severe as what I experienced when my romantic relationship ended. I caution you to avoid replacing the gap in your life caused by your ex with someone else, even if you consider him or her to just be a friend. I had to learn the hard way that even friendships can be unhealthy if they are not in their proper places in our hearts.

Although I am unable to date casually, I have friends who are able to do so. They do not get overly attached to their dates and are not in shambles when the dating does not lead to a relationship. If you fall into this category, be Spirit led regarding whom you date. Practice learning from your past mistakes and make better decisions regarding the type of person you choose. I highly recommend *Boundaries in Dating* by Dr. Henry Cloud and Dr. John Townsend. This book offers sound wisdom on dating and also being a healthy person who fosters healthy relationships with others. For a courtship perspective, I recommend reading *Choosing God's Best* by Dr. Don Raunikar. This book teaches that courtship can be an effective method of guarding one's heart and waiting on God to choose your spouse.

Courtship is different than dating in that the purpose is solely intended to see whether two people are compatible for marriage. The purpose of dating is to enjoy the other person for that moment. While dating, the couple does not discuss long-term commitment during the initial stages of the relationship, unlike in courtship. Courtship also includes boundaries, accountability, and limited one-on-one time. The purpose of the boundaries is to guard both parties' hearts so that if the courtship does not lead to marriage, the breakup will not be as difficult to heal from.

My personal belief is that the purpose of dating is to see whether you are compatible with that person for marriage, and therefore I prefer the concept of courtship. I am learning in my singleness that marriage is a huge responsibility and requires a tremendous amount of selflessness. There is a reason the divorce rate in the church rivals that of the divorce rate outside the church. Marriage is hard work! During this time of singleness, I'm finding that other relationships can help teach me about the work needed in a marriage. There are covenant friendships and family relationships in my life that challenge me to love selflessly, as Christ loves the church, just as we are required to do in marriage. I have been given ample opportunity to practice maturity, forgiveness, and unconditional love in the nonromantic relationships in my life. By taking time to develop these qualities, I now have them to rely on when the right person comes along.

I encourage you to invest time and energy in the other relationships in your life. Doing this not only helps you prepare for marriage, but I also guarantee you will receive healing from being surrounded by people who love and accept you.

Reflection Questions

1. What is your understanding of dating versus courtship?
2. If you choose to date, which boundaries will you have in place to guard your heart?
3. Which factors do you feel should be in place to let you know you are healed and ready to move on?

CHAPTER 9

FINDING TRUE LOVE

While growing up I esteemed marriage. Having been raised in a single-parent home, I saw the challenges my mom faced doing everything alone, and I did not want that plight. So I dove heart first into the first relationship that showed me promise. I was full of emotion and used very little wisdom. I was searching for true love and believed I had found it, when in reality I was simply misguided regarding what true love was. Little did I know True Love was searching for me and used my heartbreak to reveal Himself: God is love (1 John 4:8). There is no one on the face of this planet who can love us more than He does. He is our Heavenly Father and paid a serious price to call us His children. Additionally Christ did not just die to save us from damnation; He also came to restore and make us whole—by His wounds we are healed (Isa. 53:5). That means, as His children, we are entitled to be healed. This entitlement is not the self-based entitlement rooted in pride—it is our inheritance offered to us so that we can soar high above the pain and hurt of this world.

Often we believe we need someone to complete us. I believed this lie for a long time. I kept looking for completion in relationships, friendships, jobs, and so on...until finally I realized that everything this side of Heaven is temporary. There is nothing physical and tangible that will last beyond this life. The depths of the longing of my soul can be fulfilled only by the One who made my soul. That means a relationship or marriage never will ultimately satisfy, because it can exist only on this side of Heaven. It may temporarily offer me enjoyment, but identity and purpose can be found only in a relationship with the One who exists outside of time. I have not "arrived," but I continue to practice walking in these truths as I progressively move forward in my life's journey.

It took me years to heal from brokenheartedness. I can't give you a day when I woke up and said, "Today is the day I no longer hurt from this pain." I can, however, say that I no longer hurt from that pain today.

In life the journey is just as important as the destination. I hope that I have encouraged you in your journey and helped you believe that the pain you cur-rently are experiencing will end. There will be a day when you will look back and see how everything you've experienced has given you wisdom and knowledge, not only in the area of relationships but also hopefully regarding yourself and your Creator.

If you have not experienced God as your first love and know you need Him to help you through this time as well as to discover your purpose in Him, you can recite the following prayer:

Lord Jesus, I believe that You are the Son of God and that You are God. I believe that You died on the cross for my sins and that You not only offer eternal life but also offer healing and wholeness for all who believe in You. I receive You into my heart and ask that You would be Lord over my life. Please teach me how to fol-low You and, in doing so, to walk in freedom, healing, and wholeness. Thank You for the fact that all who call on Your name are saved (Rom. 10:13). Thank You for making me a part of Your family (Rom. 8:15). Amen.

MANTRA

You, (Your name), are fearfully and wonderfully made. The Alpha and Omega, the Eternal One, desires you. He desired you before you were born and hid you in His heart. He wanted you so badly that He created you for His good pleasure. He is pleased with you because you are His. He smiles upon you, and His heart races at the thought of you. You. Are. *Amazing*. You don't need a man or woman to validate you or to *need* you. To make you *feel* amazing. You *are* amazing, in and of yourself, just because Christ made you to be. You don't have to be in a relationship to feel alive or to feel successful. You have so many gifts and talents in you, many of which are being manifested in this season of your life. There is so much wrapped up in you that makes you great! You are great because your Father is great. You are strong and confident. God is the lover of your soul. Love yourself the way He loves you today.

PRAYER

Father, I pray that You would help me love myself the way that You love me. Perfect love casts out all fear (1 John 4:18). I know Your love will cast out the fear of my not being in a relationship and of not being enough if I am not in a relationship. I am more than enough. I am all that You wanted me to be, and I have exceeded Your expectations. You see me, and You are in awe.

Thank You, Father, for Your kindness toward me and for helping me see myself the way that You see me. Life is not about having a man or woman; it is about You and me. It is about the life that You purposed to manifest in me in the earth.

CPSIA information can be obtained
at www.ICGtesting.com
Printed in the USA
LVOW03s0349290917
550506LV00019B/638/P